MW00682947

Georgia
O'Keeffe

2003 POCKET CALENDAR

Pomegranate

Georgia O'Keeffe
Catalog No. F716

Published by Pomegranate Communications, Inc.
Box 6099, Rohnert Park, California 94927
800-227-1428

Front cover image:
Jimson Weed, 1936–37
Oil on linen, 177.8 x 212.1 cm (70 x 83½ in.)
Indianapolis Museum of Art
Gift of Eli Lilly and Company

Cover design by Gina Bostian
Printed in Korea

ISBN 0-7649-1949-0

All astronomical data supplied in this calendar are expressed in
Greenwich Mean Time (GMT).

Moon phases and American, Canadian, and U.K. holidays are noted.

Born near sun Prairie, Wisconsin, Georgia O'Keeffe (1887–1986) became the first female painter in America to win unanimous respect from both critics and the public. This giant of twentieth-century art carried the powerful simplicity of the prairie with her forever, always striving to capture the essence of a subject, both in spirit and in form. The twelve paintings presented in this calendar pay tribute to the eloquence of her work.

While visiting friends in Taos, New Mexico, in 1929, O'Keeffe fell in love with the beauty of the land, eventually moving to the state and devoting her energy to portraying the color and mystery of the Southwestern mountains and desert. Producing more than 2,000 paintings in her lifetime, Georgia O'Keeffe left a legacy of artistic vision that will forever be treasured.

White Pansy, 1927

Oil on canvas, 91.8 x 76.5 cm (36 x 30 in.)
© The Cleveland Museum of Art
Bequest of Georgia O'Keeffe 1987.139

january

S	M	T	W	T	F	S
			1	2	3	4
5	6	7	8	9	10	11
12	13	14	15	16	17	18
19	20	21	22	23	24	25
26	27	28	29	30	31	

30 *mon*

---

31 *tue*

NEW YEAR'S DAY   **1** *wed*

hairset

BANK HOLIDAY (SCOTLAND)
NEW MOON   **2** *thu*

Bob brings groc.

---

3 *fri*

Coffee. 9 a.m.
call Kim, Febe, D.Penfield

---

4 *sat*

Ken Keall. Bob & Chris
here. Sun. Tea.

---

5 *sun*

january Call Sheri
Order 3 Rx

mon 6
_____

tue 7
Call Amy H.
Bob shop for me, Rx etc
Waltz leads
Peter clean
_____

wed 8
hairset
_____

thu 9
_____

fri 10   FIRST QUARTER
_____

sat 11
_____

sun 12
BJ call tell re car
trouble + Amy hurt
bf of this OK.
Sunday Tea

Benedict Arnold
Call Bill

pre Bible study

13 mon

visit w/ Marianne, also a new
residents (Elizabeth and ? ?
visit w/ Helen Scinta 1 hr.

14 tue

Residents meet. Call some
people. Visit Tammy 1 hr.
Jail New

MARTIN LUTHER KING JR.'S BIRTHDAY

15 wed

Jean call - love y! she's
starting school - Helen
Scinta visit, Harriet

16 thu

Current Events
Quiet day

17 fri

Coffee, Call M Anderson,
D, Evans'. Play bingo, win!
$5.00

FULL MOON

18 sat

Church, Bob & Chris visit
Sun Tea

19 sun

january *Sue's News*
Chris ship zoome

mon 20

Talk w/ Marianne re
salary

tue 21

x'nd class for 2/P5 + St. Mi
renew Time
✓ Visit D. Purfield
Freshman + students
Peter, Jean

Call Purfield
Hurst
Current Events

thu 23

Call Sheri
J. Locke — 2:30
Chris take me to *anis*

fri 24

Coffee 9 a m
Bingo 1 p m
Listen to tape "Nature's
Symphony"

sat 25

3 p m Sun. Tea
Church 11 a m

sun 26 Bob + Chris visit eve

Letter from Pat Teague
Exercise class to prevent
falls - very good!
Call Amy H.

27 mon

Call Pat Teague
visit Penfield

28 tue

apt. cleaned.
send ck. to Mercy Health
Jessie clean ($18⁰⁰)

29 wed

Haircut
Birthday party
Current Events

30 thu

2 pm Hangman
Have been re-reading
Abigail Adams bio

31 fri

Ben Hur (half) Fri.
"coffee & doughnuts" 9 am   Sat pm
NEW MOON Columbia explodes!

1 sat

Church " am
Tea 3 pm

Bob & Chris brought
dinner - great!

2 sun

february

S	M	T	W	T	F	S
						1
2	3	4	5	6	7	8
9	10	11	12	13	14	15
16	17	18	19	20	21	22
23	24	25	26	27	28	

3 mon

Chris phap for me
Call BJ re Lungeroop
Straighten files

4 tue

Activity meet. Tub & clean
Lifeline meet. It ol re
Talk to Josie
Recpt of tables

5 wed

hairset
Recave pictures of kid from
Amy H. & letter & bag from
Fran. 3:30 pm — sunroom
        current events

6 thu

Call/order Rx. Chris got
Rx. Wash 1 load

7 fri

Upset stomach, did not
go to Sat a.m. coffee
Better by eve.

8 sat

Church 11 a m
Tea 3 pm

FIRST QUARTER

9 sun

february

Try to straighten bank & credit business.

mon 10
Call Sheri
Sidney Poitier bio
2 Actors "Blue Babies"

tue 11
Talk w/ Amy H.
Valentine party

wed 12
Read Kewanee lit.
Jessie Dean

LINCOLN'S BIRTHDAY

thu 13
Beauty shop
Current events

fri 14
Bill & Mary D. call
B J call
Rereading "John Adams"

VALENTINE'S DAY

Coffee & doughnuts

sat 15

sun 16
Church
Ina call
visit Helen S (she fell)
3pm Tea

FULL MOON

Bob & Chris brought supper

Call Helen L.

february

PRESIDENTS' DAY

17 *mon*

Call Helen L.

18 *tue*

Bea & I have coffee
Call D. Purfield
Sheri call, tell about thyroid

19 *wed*

Lunch w/ D. Purfield

20 *thu*

Birthday party

21 *fri*

Launder clothes, change
bed, "Of Mice & Men."

WASHINGTON'S BIRTHDAY

22 *sat*

Church
Tea 3 p.m.
LAST QUARTER B & call

23 *sun*

Dr Wisely 2 pm

mon 24

Walk 10"

tue 25

apt. cleaned
coffee w/Helen

wed 26

Hair set & cut
Current Events

thu 27

send ck to Detroit Pub. T
talk to people in lobby.
Bea get me coffee.
fri 28   visit Penfield

9 am coffee
call TBC
reg message Seals.
sat 1   Renners

Church
3 pm Tea
Chris get my groc.
sun 2

march

S	M	T	W	T	F	S
						1
2	3	4	5	6	7	8
9	10	11	12	13	14	15
16	17	18	19	20	21	22
23	24	25	26	27	28	29
30	31					

Green Oak Leaves, 1923

Oil on canvas mounted on wood, 30.5 x 22.9 cm (12 x 9 in.)
Collection of The Newark Museum
Bequest of Miss Cora Louise Hartshorn, 1958, 58.168

Bible class

march Call Stein (sick w. cold
" Helen - noon pair
TV stein re Drexel w.

mon 3   NEW MOON

wash 1 load
visit Helen. Chas brug
more groc & visit

tue 4

visit Bea - Charles died
activities meeting
ask Wed. services
Call Fairfield

wed 5   ASH WEDNESDAY

1 soff Haircut
flowers sit in part of inspiration
optimal Health - 1 hr.

thu 6 Current Events - no one
came

Call Richard Herod
Lv. message Stein
dep $83.70 Order PJ's

fri 7 "Greek Watung"

9 am coffee
Call David, Fran
Dinner w/ amy & B J

sat 8

Church
nap, almost missed
Tea at 3 pm
amy & call

sun 9

Residents meet.
Bible study
get Rx

10 mon

Walk 10"
Sherv call

11 tue

walk 15" & go hurt
PBS - Dinah Shore
Jessie Allen

12 wed

Beauty shop 10 am.
visit Helen S. Walk 15"
3 Men & a Tenor Sat.

13 thu

Joe entertain
"Taking Care of Baby"

14 fri

Wash 1 load
"The Quiet Man" - good
Irish movie

15 sat

Church 11 am
HC 3 pm
Dinner w/Chris Robt.

16 sun

march

mon 17

Sue's News
St. Pat's party
Bible study

ST. PATRICK'S DAY
PURIM (BEGINS AT SUNSET)

tue 18

shop 12-2 p.m.
for groceries
Looks like war!

FULL MOON

wed 19

Peter clean
Write Union Planters
ask to cash CD

thu 20

Wed. Calls for Tammy
Call Bet, get cash
Mail *Sunset*
WAR!!

fri 21

Call Amy Herod - to Mersey
watch TV - War
Helen in hosp.

VERNAL EQUINOX 1:00 A.M. (GMT)

Coffee, doughnuts

sat 22

Ed Libs died

sun 23

Church 11 a m
Tea - 3 p m
Call Bob, Sheri
B & call

Walk in hall, visit
R. Saunders, H. Scinta   *march*
Robt. get money from bank.
Bill call - Voltarin
            Bible study   **24** mon

Walk in hall, go to ~~Pat~~
Tea w/ Pat. Nap 45" did
      up + stomach
LAST QUARTER   not eat supper. **25** tue

Better Wed. a.m.
Calls re mammogram
J. + see Ellen
                           26 wed

Perm   Call BJ   Walk 15"
current Events   BJ birt
birth party
Call Helen   **27** thu

Laundry   visit
Mail ck. Bov et   aspasia
coffee w/ Bea
exam J. Locke   **28** fri

coffee 9 a m   Amy H. call
Jan call
Call Helen.   **29** sat

Church   Call Helen
Bea 3 p.m.
Bab + Kris bring dinner
MOTHERING SUNDAY (U.K.)   great!
SUMMER TIME BEGINS (U.K.)   **30** sun

mon 31

Walk Bill, study
~~Wash~~ shadsbergs
Gas in stomach from
that old? *(unclear)*
Feel better
today

tue 1   NEW MOON

Whitaker for taxes. Iver
Chris brub abfs. Talk to
Bobby, visit Helen

wed 2   activities meet.

Wed. Bea, coffee. Lo. menu
for Bill, Fran call. Call Sheri
Beauty shop.

thu 3   Inspiration. visit Purfield

Mail IRS. Coffee w/ Bea
Look as the the old, no
be ludwig

fri 4

Coffee, 9 - 10:30
visit Betty, Lael, eve. 6 - 8 pm
? Ruth Thompson
Piano recital + grad!

sat 5   Bill call re Voltaren

Church 11 am. Tea 3 pm?
Call Purfield, Bob, Bg. Tabor

sun 6   DAYLIGHT SAVING TIME BEGINS

a p r i l

S	M	T	W	T	F	S
		1	2	3	4	5
6	7	8	9	10	11	12
13	14	15	16	17	18	19
20	21	22	23	24	25	26
27	28	29	30			

Purple Petunias, 1925

Oil on canvas, 40.3 x 33 cm (15⅞ x 13 in.)
Collection of The Newark Museum
Bequest of Miss Cora Louise Hartshorn, 1958, 58.167

april Wash / load
Res.-meet.

---

mon 7

chris stop by

---

tue 8

Saddam toppled!
Jesse clean
Got RX

---

wed 9 "Peter, Paul, etc." **FIRST QUARTER**

Haircut
Inspiration Hr.
Current Events

---

thu 10

a.m. stomach upset - taking
it easy. Drank coke, so
by 7 p.m. much better

---

fri 11

went to coffee 9 a.m.
Got RX at pharmacy

---

sat 12

Church 9 a.m
Tea 3 p.m

---

sun 13 **PALM SUNDAY**

shop groc, Sheri call.
Bible class

april

14 mon

Call Amy H.
Musicians didn't
come — we waited *Pay taxes*
an hr.!

15 tue

Peter clean Bea gave
me coffee. Call Barnes,
Evans

FIRST NIGHT OF PASSOVER
FULL MOON

16 wed

Call Renner
Haircut

SECOND NIGHT OF PASSOVER

17 thu

1:30 pm. Good Fri. service
walk & visit Helen
~~Good Fri. service 1:30 pm~~

GOOD FRIDAY

18 fri

9:30 - coffee
1 pm - harp concert - great!
Jan L. call
Lv. m essage for Bill Bob

19 sat

Chris & I to cousin Mary
for brunch — great! Bob
sutures for finale

EASTER SUNDAY

20 sun

april *Helen & ill Today*
Res. meet re tags on doc
Sue's news. Dorothy & I spend
time w/ Helen

mon 21   EASTER MONDAY (CANADA, U.K.)

wash / load
Helen is better!

tue 22   EARTH DAY

Peter clean
meet re volunteers
Play bingo wed eve

wed 23   LAST QUARTER

Hairset, Chris visit
Bill call
thu 24 *Call Sheri . birthd*
~~Birth party~~

Birth party

fri 25

Wash / load
coffee 9 a m

sat 26

11 a m Church, 2 ea - 3 p m
Bob visit

sun 27

Hildreth - lighthouses
Haugman - Dave april/may

28 mon

Give M? bio, visit Helen
call Amy H.

29 tue

Party for recognition of
volunteers
Chris visit — nice!

30 wed

Hamet activity meeting
Betty L. play piano eve.

NEW MOON   **1** thu

Straighten desk, discard
watch Bob Hope 100, Berth-
address birth cards Bill,
Sheri

2 fri

Wash 1 load
Coffee 9 a.m. To Huron
Woods w/ Bob, Chris, et al

3 sat

Detroit Opera:
Don Giovanni,
wonderful!
Bill call, talk to **4** sun
Minnie, D. Stein call

White Flower on Red Earth, No. 1, 1943

Oil on canvas, 66 x 76.8 cm (26 x 30¼ in.)
Collection of The Newark Museum
Purchase 1946 John J. O'Neill Bequest Fund, 46.157

m a y

S	M	T	W	T	F	S
				1	2	3
4	5	6	7	8	9	10
11	12	13	14	15	16	17
18	19	20	21	22	23	24
25	26	27	28	29	30	31

Chris shop for me
Volunteers meet.

CINCO DE MAYO
BANK HOLIDAY (U.K.)
5 *mon*

Bill's birthday

6 *tue*

Jessie clean
Mother's Day party

7 *wed*

Haircut. Inspiration Hour.
Current Events

8 *thu*

Get Rx, Talk to Dr. Stein,
et al.

FIRST QUARTER
9 *fri*

Call Fran (her birth)
Open House & bazaar,
Call Sheri, Amy H. (vi. message)

10 *sat*

a Wonderful Day — Amy Ben
bring lunch & go to church w/me
2nd lovely flowers. Chris
& Bob come later

MOTHER'S DAY
11 *sun*

may

Res. meetings.
k. tags
Sing-along

mon 12

Bob & Chris visit, bring
groc + $
visit Easter
tue 13 call Ann Barnes, B J

Willie clean
Sit on patio 1 hr.
nice day!
wed 14 Al - slides of china

Hairset
3 pm current events
Bob stop w/ groc
thu 15 Helen visit (depressed

"What Is it?" program Sat
Shirley Temple movie
wash 1 load
fri 16   FULL MOON

coffee 9:15 10:15 - 1 hr visit
nap 1 hr.   w/ D. Penfield
sat 17   ARMED FORCES DAY

church 11 am
Tea 3 pm. Lovely visit
w/ Ina, also gifts
sun 18

Amy & Ben calif - new
bird "Lily"
Lyn's Nems
Sit outside 1 hr. - lovely
day.

may

VICTORIA DAY (CANADA)   **19** mon

Call Sherie.
Set Rx

Ai talk re time 6:30 p.m.   **20** tue

Jessie clean
Pain very bad today
walk 15 a.m.
call Amy - Sean sick
walk 15" - p.m.   **21** wed

Haircut. Talk to Betty L.
Call Chris. Rest 1/2 hr.

22 thu

birth party
watch Anika

LAST QUARTER   **23** fri

Chris/Robt. visit p.m., discard
files.
P.M. eve - J. Carson old TV shows

24 sat

Church
3. p.m. Tea
8. p.m. Mem. Concert - good!
B.J call
25 sun

may/june

*Line+ day. Chris's
visit. Read Barry school
book*

mon 26

*Talk to Matrone re tags.
Discard/hang clothes
Chris came for lunch
Music Makers*

tue (27) *R's birthday*

*~~Talk to~~ Laundry.
sit outside 45" — lovely day
Will clean.*

wed 28

hairset

thu 29

GWTW ene ½

fri 30

*GWTW - last ½
Bob + Chris helped a lot*

sat 31

*church
Tea 3 pm
Bell call*

sun 1

j u n e

S	M	T	W	T	F	S
1	2	3	4	5	6	7
8	9	10	11	12	13	14
15	16	17	18	19	20	21
22	23	24	25	26	27	28
29	30					

Dee Mar. 28.

A Sunflower from Maggie, 1937

Oil on canvas, 40.6 x 50.8 cm (16 x 20 in.)
Alfred Stieglitz Collection, Bequest of Georgia O'Keeffe 1987.542
Courtesy, Museum of Fine Arts, Boston

june _walk outside_
lovely day

mon 2

(Return things to D. Purf

tue 3 Jessie clean)

(Busy day. Talk to Prophyt visit
Leah, see Therapy Dog, Ann &
Toby) activity meet. Botanical
lecture. China lecture
wed 4 Chris & Robert stop by

walk Haircut. call Sheri
10" get Rx (Talk after 3 p.m. to
Dorothy)
thu 5 Current Events
Chris shop for me

Lovely day, sit outsi
wash, load change
bed. watch J. Gleason.
fri 6 Robert & I write & mail check

Coffee 9 a.m.
walk around Village
+ watch part of Red Wings
sat (Net Worth) movie FIRST QUARTER

Church, birth party
Aspasia. Tea 3 p.m. —
amy to call — all fine
sun 8

Resident meeting
Walk around building

June

9 mon

Dr. Shelton, Dr. Wisely
Bob take me, get Rx

10 tue

room cleaned

11 wed

& at
hairset, Music p.m.
Current Events 6:30
Call Betty S.

12 thu

D. Penfield call
Unity Pat Teague
with Thin Man
wash / load

13 fri

Father's day party
Call Fran, messages
" Tom Sealy - he had accident
Set outside
FLAG DAY
FULL MOON   9 am - Coffee.

14 sat

Church, Ice 3 p m
Chris & Bob here

FATHER'S DAY

15 sun

Louise call

june

see Sue's News "Jazz"
watch Ken Burns
at outside 1 hr

mon 16

Observe those painting
a banner

tue 17

Phys. Therapy 11 a m

wed 18

hairset
Fran call
Chris call
Robt. call

thu 19

birth party
Call Mary Dean
" Fran

fri 20

Coffee 9:15
Talk to Bill
D Busfield visit — play piano
Listen Betty L.
walk around

sat 21 LAST QUARTER
SUMMER SOLSTICE 7:10 p.m. (GMT)

Church
Betty L. visit
3 p m — Tea
Bab + Chris visit

sun 22

Chris + I walk

sit on patio — w/ Betty L.
then in lobby

june

23 mon

& change bed
Laundry. B.J. call
Chris ate lunch w/ me
sit on patio

24 tue

apt. cleaned
& Locke exam (O.K.)
Sit on patio, nap
Amy L. call, Lauretta

25 wed

hairset, go to Inspiration Dr.
bed & breakfast
Sit outside 1/2 hr.
6:30 pm — Current Events

26 thu

walk) 20" all halls
rest
Chris' recital, lovely visit
w/ ann, et al

27 fri

walk outside, look at
Betty's herbs. Coffee 9 a.m.
Jean call. Rest. Watch part of
Music Man

28 sat

Church. Coffee
3 pm Coffee
visit Helen
walk around Village
NEW MOON Bob & Chris here
bring groc.

29 sun

june/july

mon 30
Tabor call
Kim call - great!
Eric James b. 6 2-0
wash, wael
Sit outside pm. lovely day.

tue 1   CANADA DAY (CANADA)

wed 2
apt. cleaned
activity meeting
current events

thu 3
Haircut
walk outside us/ Betty
all around ~~to~~ Esther
building

fri 4   INDEPENDENCE DAY
Walk inside. Bob visit
Sit outside, watch rain
clouds
Concert from
Wash- D.C.

sat 5
Coffee 9 am
Quiet day

sun 6
Church
Tea 3 p.m.
Chris & Bob visit
7 p.m - Scrabble

july

S	M	T	W	T	F	S
		1	2	3	4	5
6	7	8	9	10	11	12
13	14	15	16	17	18	19
20	21	22	23	24	25	26
27	28	29	30	31		

White Flower, 1929

Oil on canvas, 76.5 x 91.8 cm (30⅛ x 36⅛ in.)
© The Cleveland Museum of Art
Hinman B. Hurlbut Collection 2162.1930

walk 10" good!

july

call Sheri - good!
watch Bataan Death

mon 7 March. Order O my

1 p m Trivia
sit outside 15"
visit Helen

tue 8

apt cleaned
Ing visit - great!
get Rx

wed 9 Current Events

walk outside 10"
piano recital
haircut

thu 10

laundry
BJ visit

fri 11

9 a m coffee
sit in patio - lovely!
Bob visit. Watch Lake or the Field

sat 12 walk 10"

church
Tea 3 p m (5-) - even.
walk 15"
Bill call re my going
to Tucson

sun 13

I call Bob to make pla

visit w/ R. Thompson a.m
Lovely visit w/ Chris p.m ~ 13 July
Call Ken Kaufman

BANK HOLIDAY (N. IRELAND)   14 mon

Walk. Fran call
load laundry
Watch Wimbledon & Ifield on TV   15 tue

making plans to go to
AZ. 3:30-
Concert - Ruth's g.d. sing   16 wed

Call Bill & Bob re
Get Fit class, Beauty shop
plans.
Nap. Root beer floats 6 p.m ~ 3.38 p.m   17 thu
Bob call. Amy H. call

Get Fit. Shuffleboard a.m.
Nap. Sat on patio w/ Jane   18 fri

9:30 - Coffee
watch bus go to Art Fair
visit in lobby
visit Winnie
Nap   19 sat

Church
3 p.m. Tea

20 sun

july

walk outside, lovely
after rain

mon 21   LAST QUARTER

Sue's News
nap
Walk, Trivia

tue 22

wed 23

walk
Current Events
visit Esther eve

thu 24

Haircut
10 am. strength training
get Rx

fri 25

walk.
birth party
Fran & Jason visit

sat 26

laundry
walk
9 am - coffee

sun 27

Breakfast at Chris & Bob's
Fran & Jason there
getting ready to go to AZ
Sba @ 3 p.m.

walk
nap

28 mon

Grace call
Get ready to travel

NEW MOON   **29** tue

Fly to Tucson / Phoenix

Wonderful visit   **30** wed
w/ Dian, Bill, cheri, David,
Sophie, Amy, Sean, Alyssa

31 thu

1 fri

2 sat

3 sun

Cliffs Beyond Abiquiu, Dry Waterfall, 1943

Oil on canvas, 76.2 x 40.6 cm (30 x 16 in.)

august

S	M	T	W	T	F	S
					1	2
3	4	5	6	7	8	9
10	11	12	13	14	15	16
17	18	19	20	21	22	23
24	25	26	27	28	29	30
31						

CIVIC HOLIDAY (CANADA, MOST PROVINCES)
BANK HOLIDAY (SCOTLAND)

4 *mon*

arrive St. L. today. Amy &
Ben picked me up

FIRST QUARTER

5 *tue*

Unpack, wash / load

6 *wed*

Hairset
Inspiration

7 *thu*

8 *fri*

write ches.
9:00 - coffee
visit D. Stein
But Cushion trip in Couture

9 *sat*

church
3 pm M. Lea
Reading "Granny "D"

10 *sun*

august

Res. meeting @ M.
visit Ruth T.
Esther visit here

mon 11

Podiatrist
visit on patio w/ Bob
Back hurting more

tue 12   FULL MOON

Perm + set. Jessie clean
7 p.m. Bob + Gte Hart
Hela "Gardens"

wed 13 Good visit w/ Chris

walk, Get Fit
Evelyn gave me tomato
Power off at 3 p.m.

thu 14

Power returned 9: 45 a.m.
Dinner at noon
Stein visit, also Teddy
fri 15 Call R. Thompson, R. Moss

9 a.m. - Coffee
2 p.m. - piano concert

sat 16

Church
3 p.m. Tea
Sit outside w/ Stei
sun 17 et al. Jan S. call

Back to Normal - almost!

nap
Finish "Sanny "D"
Jane Pauley A & E   **18** mon

Sign new contract
wash / load
Helen visit visit   **19** tue

Willie clean
call Fred
Carol Brodbeck - personality
LAST QUARTER F. Sinatra - good! **20** wed

Hairset
preparation &c.
Willie clean
visit Bea, return book   **21** thu

2-yr. anniversary -
              great!
                                     22 fri

9 a.m. coffee
2 p.m. musical program
                                     23 sat

Church
3 p.m. Tea
Carris & Bob here
                                     24 sun

august

Think I have a compression fracture
Call Dr. not there
Reading James Herriot

mon 25   BANK HOLIDAY (U.K. EXCEPT SCOTLAND)

Red Hot meet/lunch.
Call Dr. again
Call Amy, lv message

tue 26

Will clean. Dr. Bridget
speak — home visits
7 pm as you Lake St

wed 27   NEW MOON

hairset
Observe Mars great

thu 28

birth party

fri 29

Amy H call
Fran + Jason call
9 am — coffee
Mrs. R here

sat 30

Fran + Jason here

sun 31

september

S	M	T	W	T	F	S
	1	2	3	4	5	6
7	8	9	10	11	12	13
14	15	16	17	18	19	20
21	22	23	24	25	26	27
28	29	30				

Chris R., Sua, Mike, Ben/a, all
to has ball game Cleveland
Jason's father played handball
Nice visit w/ Jason, Fran & m on
Sun. aug. 31

Jimson Weed, 1936–1937

Oil on linen, 177.8 × 212.1 cm (70 × 83½ in.)
Indianapolis Museum of Art
Gift of Eli Lilly and Company

september rain

Order Rx

tue 2

Jessie clean
"Reading "Art for
wed 3 Dummies"   FIRST QUARTER
3:30 Current Events
& Call D Purfield, Bill, Sheri,
Evans (lv message)
Chris get Rx
thu 4 Nurse & Insp. Hr.
Not a good day dizzy

Better today

fri 5 "chicago"—very good
4 a.m. coffee
2 loads laundry
Chris & Bob visit
sat 6 Amy call + good!

Grandparents Day
New Residents Day
Church - 11 a.m.
sun 7 Frazier call

visit R. Mosher to see walker
Taichi

8 mon

---

write Pat Teague
next
Linda pick up ironing
write checks

9 tue

Will clean
call D & B for Sept 3 appen-
attend Lottie's presentation
FULL MOON on silver

10 wed

---

haircut
take 2nd day 1 p.m.

11 thu

Ben & Amy call
I call Stephanie
Buy new silver walker

12 fri

---

walk around bldg.
w/Betty L. - ice cream
play bingo
1 p.m.

13 sat

---

church
did not go to tea - visit
w/ Chris

14 sun

september

mon 15 straighten clothes on hangers. visit Beg. she gave me "Chicken Soup" nap 1½ hrs.

call: Seals, Renner
Chris & I to Dr. Wisely

tue 16

Get 25¢ stamps from office
1:30 exercise
3:30 Current Events

wed 17 6 p.m. visit R. Thompson
Esther & Betty, too

walk, hairset

thu 18   LAST QUARTER

Put things away, rest

fri 19 "My Fair Lady" party

sun Lovely day, sit out in
9 a.m. (coffee 9 — 10:30)
porch party. Call Amy

sat 20 My Fair Lady (2 nd)
Church
3 p.m. Tea
walk outside after

sun 21 dinner

Put things away!
visit w/ Chris during september
bake sale
Look for pillow

22 mon

strength training
personal history
BJ call

23 tue

Return book to Bob in
lobby. Will clean room.
Echocardiogram
Hylke's talk re Laos

24 wed

haircut, visit Ruth T.
Music / appreciation

Jan call. I call her
laundry 2 loads
Calls for Tammy

25 thu

Zion singers

26 fri

9 a m - coffee
write Coffey
walk 2 halls

Read Blair
book. Betty
bring muffins

27 sat

Church 11 a m
Tea 3 p m
visit Helen, see men
Chris & Bob etc, love
shop Safeway

28 sun

september/october

Elam by J. Locke
Sue's news

mon 29

Red Hat Society meet
+ lunch.

tue 30

Get Rx (Order cosmetics
from Michelle
activities meeting *Fri*
B J call

wed 1 J call - amy no answer
Sheri she's well
Jessie clean hairset
Fran call 'great!

thu 2   FIRST QUARTER

walk hours, nap

fri 3

9am coffee

sat 4

11 am church
3 p.m. Tea
sun 5 Bob visit   YOM KIPPUR (BEGINS AT SUNSET)

october

S	M	T	W	T	F	S
			1	2	3	4
5	6	7	8	9	10	11
12	13	14	15	16	17	18
19	20	21	22	23	24	25
26	27	28	29	30	31	

Oak Leaves, Pink and Gray, 1929

Oil on canvas, 84.1 x 45.7 cm (33⅛ x 18 in.)
Collection Frederick R. Weisman Art Museum,
University of Minnesota, Minneapolis. Museum Purchase.

october

Call Tabor
write Evans
Call Chris

mon 6 Watch "Horatio's Drive"

Not feeling well. nap
Took second oxygentin ". 15

tue 7

Rereading Oxford dictionary
sit outside, walk   Nap (story
to Hylke   (almost
                          late for dinner)

wed 8 Rachel clean

dessert, get fit
Trivia

thu 9

Jan call - she's coming
Sat. I
Bob call Bob 7 p.m.
                    Laura brought
fri 10   cookie

Dana Ruthie here a.m.
slept visit! 9 a.m. - Tea
Chris also visit, Lawrence
sat 11 3 loads. Amy call re
Davids birthday Richard R&R
call him. Church
3 p.m. - Tea
sun 12 supper w/ Robt & Chris

COLUMBUS DAY

Exercise 10 a.m.
Res. meeting 10:30 a.m.
Lv. message Evans   october
Call Heroa. Walk hall, sit
                outside
COLUMBUS DAY OBSERVED
THANKSGIVING DAY (CANADA)   Reading   **13** mon
"The Professor & the Madman"
Write Amy, et al. send money
BJ call. Walk halls
Dr. 9 a.m. strength training   **14** tue
Dr. Shelton foot care
Jessie clean. visit w/ Helen
PM - nap. Current Events

15 wed

Walk, Exercise 10 a.m.
Beauty shop. Birth party

16 thu

Call Dr. W, verify appt. for
flu shot 9 a.m. Sat. 15th
Call Mary Dean   **17** fri

flu shot. 9 a.m. coffee
walk halls

LAST QUARTER   **18** sat

Chris take me to BJ Amy
lovely day. 3 pm Tea coffee
Ken K call. Walk hall for
Jan S. call. Lv. message
        Mary S. birth.   **19** sun

slept late. call Pharm
re josamat. Bible
study. walk hills.
Listen to "Butterfly".

october

mon 20

walk hills. Call Chris
call Herod. a m + p m

tue 21

Room cleaned. bed on deck
Walk hole. Musical program
7 p m. Meth. Church

wed 22

Hair
Reading "Prof & Madman."

thu 23

1:30. Hangman
3:00. Music appreciation

fri 24   UNITED NATIONS DAY

9 a m Choir
write Ricard
Laundry/food
walk

sat 25   NEW MOON

Church. Tea 3 p m.
B J call

sun 26   DAYLIGHT SAVING TIME ENDS
                              SUMMER TIME ENDS (U.K.)

Walk
Sr. Fitness
Bob call re $ in ck. acct.

27 mon

exercise 10 a.m., 1 p.m.
walk. Nap 1 hr.

28 tue

Leave message Ina
House helper clean
Hed Vet @ Huron Woods

29 wed

Hairset Exercise
Cash in tokens
Call Herod

30 thu

1:30 party Halloween
HALLOWEEN 7 p.m. Cider & 31 fri
donuts
9 a.m. coffee
walk p.m.

7 p.m. "Raintree County" 1 sat
FIRST QUARTER
Church.
2. piano recital. 3 Tea & coffee
Bob & Chris visit, shop for me
"Dr. Zivago" - not as good 2 sun
as Julia

Gate of an Adobe Church, 1929

Oil on canvas, 51 x 40.6 cm (20¹/₁₆ x 16 in.)
Carnegie Museum of Art, Pittsburgh
Gift in memory of Elisabeth Mellon Sellers from her friends 74.17
Photographer: Peter Harholdt

november

S	M	T	W	T	F	S
						1
2	3	4	5	6	7	8
9	10	11	12	13	14	15
16	17	18	19	20	21	22
23	24	25	26	27	28	29
30						

Straighten up.
This shop & visit,
walk in hall. visit Esther
"5"

3 mon

Exercise, wash 2 loads
change bed,   early
9:30. Memories 1940's
Watch "M*A*S*H"

4 tue

Late getting up.
:30 Sammys meeting
Jessie clean the Bureau &
3:00 visit w/ D. Purfield
wed nite "Romance & War"
PBS - Ernie Pyle, et al

5 wed

hairset, walk. Bill call
Talk by gardener 7 pm,
walk in halls. Call Helen,
Music appreciation
Fran call.

6 thu

Set.
9 am Coffee

7 fri

Sun. 6 pm - Bea stop by.
Roses from D. Goffe.

8 sat

Church
"Madame Butterfly"
Wonderful

9 sun

FULL MOON

3 & visit 6 pm,

november

mon 10
Res-meet 10:30 am
Calls to remind
Gary - toilet seat
visit in lobby, Hilda
rest 2 hr

tue 11
Take Chris, Hilda around
Village

wed 12
appt. w/ J - Locke 9:30 a.m.
Laura clean

thu 13
Inspiration 10:30
Hansel 11:30

fri 14
Visit Penfield 1½ hrs.
Chris. visit, bring program
7 p.m. Fam. history

sat 15
Urinary problem.
Laundry 10:30 Coffee
wash lots of bedding!

sun 16
Better today. Will call Dr.
Mon. Church. Dinner 12:30
Tea 3 p.m. Bob visit. Walk
visit Ruth T.

LAST QUARTER 17 *mon*

birthday party - cloggers.
Call Amy H.

18 *tue*

Call Ina - birthday" 2 hr
Helen stop in 15"

walk 15", 1 p m - perm 19 *wed*

get mail & coffee

20 *thu*

Put away papers, etc

21 *fri*

9 a.m. coffee

22 *sat*

Bob & Chris take me to day
Ann's b-party - lovely
have supper last, enjoy

NEW MOON 23 *sun*

Robert hangup quarters

november

"~~Life Stinks~~" Mitford
Shepherds dividing

mon 24 Nap 45" Call A. Bar.
Michal show my apt.
hairset B J & Amy call
from Florida Everglades

tue 25 ~~Spring~~ competition great
Call family for T-giving
talk to Fran 1½ hr.
"   "   Amy H. 15"

wed 26 Current Events 3:30
talk to Peters
Rachel clean, change bed
Write Bea
Search for Jaguar wed.

thu 27 Helen call _____ +
Lovely day at Donald's   THANKSGIVING DAY
Sort thru videotapes
Mary d. call - nice.

fri 28
9:30 am - Coffee

sat 29

Amy K & I to church
1 pm dinner
3 pm
3:30 Bob visit

sun 30   FIRST QUARTER

december

S	M	T	W	T	F	S
	1	2	3	4	5	6
7	8	9	10	11	12	13
14	15	16	17	18	19	20
21	22	23	24	25	26	27
28	29	30	31			

Calla Lily on Grey, 1928

Oil on canvas, 81 × 43.2 cm (31⅞ × 17 in.)
Gift of the William H. Lane Foundation 1990.431
Courtesy, Museum of Fine Arts, Boston

write thank you Len

december launder 1 load

order Fagomax & Neurontin

Listen Betty play plans

mon 1 Bea died Today

Call Helen

tue 2

1 pm Activity meet

3:30 Current Events

wed 3

no hairset

Pat's class 10:30 1 Nap

thu 4 Madonna U. - Nancy ?

Pam call, D return call,

fri 5

9 am - coffee

11:30 - hairset

visit Helen & Ann

sat 6 Call Betty L. - she's very sick

Ina call

11 am - Church

sun 7 1:30 brunch

3:00 Tea   3 pm

Chris visit. Call B. Leach

Residents meeting
Stan & Lollie visit eve.
Fran call - nice!

FULL MOON 8 mon

Podiatrist. Helen visit
Zion Singers p.m.

9 tue

Gary clean drains.
Josie clean.
7 p.m. Violinist from UGM
very good! Current Events
10 wed
3:30 Wed.

Sue - ck. temp, b.p.
call Betty L. Ira visit. gift
wash, load. amaryllis 11 thu
this being bread
birth party

12 fri

9 a.m - coffee. call Betty L.

13 sat

Church. Saddam
tea party captured

14 sun

2:15 p.m. Tea w/ Tammy & Pat

december

1 p.m. Sue's News

mon 15 Sheri call. I call Amy &.

Bob call, Walk hall.

tue 16   LAST QUARTER

Jessie clean
Current Events

wed 17

Hairset. visit w/ Leah
She's much better!!

thu 18

Bob bring Rx

fri 19   HANUKKAH (BEGINS AT SUNSET)

Coffee Hour

sat 20   FIRST DAY OF HANUKKAH

Church
3 p.m. I help me
sun 21 Robt. help me
Fran & Jason visit
early a.m.

WINTER SOLSTICE 7:04 A.M. (GMT)

22 *mon*

NEW MOON

23 *tue*

---

24 *wed*

CHRISTMAS DAY

25 *thu*

KWANZAA BEGINS
BOXING DAY (CANADA, U.K.)

26 *fri*

---

27 *sat*

---

28 *sun*

---

december/january

mon 29

---

tue 30   FIRST QUARTER

---

wed 31

---

thu 1   NEW YEAR'S DAY

---

fri 2   BANK HOLIDAY (SCOTLAND)

---

sat 3

---

sun 4

2004

january
S	M	T	W	T	F	S
				1	2	3
4	5	6	7	8	9	10
11	12	13	14	15	16	17
18	19	20	21	22	23	24
25	26	27	28	29	30	31

february
S	M	T	W	T	F	S
1	2	3	4	5	6	7
8	9	10	11	12	13	14
15	16	17	18	19	20	21
22	23	24	25	26	27	28
29						

march
S	M	T	W	T	F	S
	1	2	3	4	5	6
7	8	9	10	11	12	13
14	15	16	17	18	19	20
21	22	23	24	25	26	27
28	29	30	31			

april
S	M	T	W	T	F	S
				1	2	3
4	5	6	7	8	9	10
11	12	13	14	15	16	17
18	19	20	21	22	23	24
25	26	27	28	29	30	

may
S	M	T	W	T	F	S
						1
2	3	4	5	6	7	8
9	10	11	12	13	14	15
16	17	18	19	20	21	22
23	24	25	26	27	28	29
30	31					

june
S	M	T	W	T	F	S
		1	2	3	4	5
6	7	8	9	10	11	12
13	14	15	16	17	18	19
20	21	22	23	24	25	26
27	28	29	30			

july
S	M	T	W	T	F	S
				1	2	3
4	5	6	7	8	9	10
11	12	13	14	15	16	17
18	19	20	21	22	23	24
25	26	27	28	29	30	31

august
S	M	T	W	T	F	S
1	2	3	4	5	6	7
8	9	10	11	12	13	14
15	16	17	18	19	20	21
22	23	24	25	26	27	28
29	30	31				

september
S	M	T	W	T	F	S
			1	2	3	4
5	6	7	8	9	10	11
12	13	14	15	16	17	18
19	20	21	22	23	24	25
26	27	28	29	30		

october
S	M	T	W	T	F	S
					1	2
3	4	5	6	7	8	9
10	11	12	13	14	15	16
17	18	19	20	21	22	23
24	25	26	27	28	29	30
31						

november
S	M	T	W	T	F	S
	1	2	3	4	5	6
7	8	9	10	11	12	13
14	15	16	17	18	19	20
21	22	23	24	25	26	27
28	29	30				

december
S	M	T	W	T	F	S
			1	2	3	4
5	6	7	8	9	10	11
12	13	14	15	16	17	18
19	20	21	22	23	24	25
26	27	28	29	30	31	

personal information

name _____

address _____

city _____ state _____ zip _____

phone _____

cell/pgr _____ fax _____

e-mail _____

in case of emergency, please notify:

name _____

address _____

city _____ state _____ zip _____

phone _____

physician's name _____

physician's phone _____

health insurance company _____

plan number _____

allergies _____

other _____

driver's license number _____

car insurance company _____

policy number _____

Pomegranate also publishes *Georgia O'Keeffe* wall, mini wall, and engagement calendars for 2003, as well as an O'Keeffe boxed notecard set, an address book, and a book of post-cards. Our products and publications include books, posters, postcards, notecards, magnets, mousepads, Knowledge Cards™, birthday books, journals, screen savers, and bookmarks. For more information or to place an order, please contact Pomegranate Communications, Inc.: 800-227-1428; www.pomegranate.com.

Available in Canada from Canadian Manda Group,
One Atlantic Avenue #105,
Toronto, Ontario M6K 3E7, Canada

Available in the U.K. and mainland Europe from
Pomegranate Europe Ltd., Fullbridge House,
Fullbridge, Maldon, Essex CM9 4LE, England

Available in Australia from Hardie Grant Books,
12 Claremont Street, South Yarra, Victoria 3141

Available in New Zealand from Randy Horwood Ltd.,
P.O. Box 32-077, Devonport, Auckland

Available in Asia (including the Middle East), Africa, and
Latin America from Pomegranate International Sales,
113 Babcombe Drive, Thornhill,
Ontario L3T 1M9, Canada